JUST
AFTER

kelly moffett

ISBN: 978-1-7337848-3-2

Director: Kareem Tayyar
Project Editor: Jeffrey Douglas
Book Design and Layout: Chan Plett

I do not know which to prefer,
The beauty of inflections
Or the beauty of innuendoes,
The blackbird whistling
Or just after.

WALLACE STEVENS

CONTENTS

WANTING A GOD IN KENTUCKY

A memory of mom drifts by disguised as tissue.
I try to read it but it is confused by the wind.

A half dozen turtles, each small as my palm.
The day shakes the sorrow from its skin.

Whose hand is on the faucet of this morning?
Every drop absorbed by field.

My language is leggy and about to dart.
A shape sometimes passes above me.

This afternoon of yawn and stretch, this little
warbler of expectation. I've given up for less.

The dog drops its image into the pond; its nose
pushes through a cloud caught in water.

A wood thrush shoves through the brush.
My hand slashes a Pin Oak's shadow.

I want a face to take the place of the sun.
I keep looking but mostly it's not there.

WHERE THE MARRIAGE IS

I wash the night out of the dinner napkin.
The floor extends under me like a wave.

Plates cover the counter like buttons.
The rain a garbled language.

I say the same bad thing.
It's clear W hears it many times.

In landscape, it is often the foliage
at the edge that is interesting.

W empties his pockets.
Stacks the day's nothing into a drawer.

Opens it only to open it again.
See there?

Where nothing changes?
It's right where I don't want to be.

LETTER NOT SENT TO MOM

Did the nose of the afternoon catch you off guard?
Did it push you into the grass?

You sang something small to the dirt.
I think it was about summer and death.

The morning stiffened on the porch.
Breathe through it, mom. Find the breath.

Take a deep breath.
Let the elevator doors of this distress close.

There is a language outside your window.
You put your hand on the glass and try to

make it out. What dangers out there, mom.

DO WHAT YOU CAN WHEN YOU CAN

The soft part of the plot
limps through an otherwise proper day.

A childhood ties itself to the dock.
There were so many pockets to stick things in.

Where are the already written pages?
The favored noise?

Out in the garage, a shelf falls.
My mouth opens then quiets
where a sentence should be.

See what the robin on her nest wonders.

Even now, as I look, I have to tell myself to look.
There's a bit of glass as well as a sun that gets bold.

Today is life. I like it that way.

LETTER NOT SENT TO W

This scene closes its curtain, dear W.
This new is so new. Full of matter that somehow

stays whole until I scoop it in my hand
and it melts clear away. The dog tunnels

with its nose, snaps at my heel. For what
is a page but what settles into margins.

Nights you pace the porch. Kick through
ice like an angry horse. I want you back.

This is where my students hear "crunch."
For them snow is snow. Each will love

perhaps a dozen times or more. Give a life of
handshakes. Take a thousand cuts. Listen to

the pattern, I tell them, before it disappears.

EARLY SPRING

On the tv I watch a man stack goat heads
into a "meat pyramid" to attract a panther.

I can no longer handle plot after mom's
dementia, so I click through this program

and that, finding even HGTV has conflict:
"how to remove this wallpaper?"

and "will two bathrooms be enough?"
Outside landscape narrates: a daffodil

lifts its new head, a young robin bops,
a bit of the dog's shaved hair breaks

from its pile and flies away.

A "DO NOT GO" POEM

I know it is one of the three poisons the world
creates: attachment. (The others being

aggression and ignorance, says
the Buddhist magazine.) The attachment

and its attendant troubles dig into my palm.

In the space between birdsong, a cow moans.
A conflict plays: will W stay or will he go?

I do not pay attention to my fear and then

I do. Next door, Chemlawn sprays. The neighbor
washes his car for the second time this week.

A line skips over and over in my head
from Strand: *this dream of flesh from moment*

to moment. And how in that poem an old man
looks at his naked body in a forest. So while

I know I will not gather like a congregant naked
in a wood or even in the neighbor's yard, I watch

as I move past the noon of my life and nothing
changes. Somewhere else, a horse rolls in a field

to shake a fly free from its neck.

AFTER THE HOT WALK

In which I can no longer walk through grass
since my fear of snakes has grown into a phobia,
I read "all sound is mantra." Right now Zeppelin
comes from W's room and a bass beats

at the neighbor's above-ground pool.
But the dog and cat settle in silence,
which I far prefer as a mantra rather
than *oh, yeah, yeah* from Zeppelin or the *boom*

boom of bass. Can what I see become sound
too? Children run around the pool in their bright
swimsuits. The gray fur of the cat. The black fur
of the dog. The swirl of paisley on the ottoman.

Yesterday, mom woke to four women hanged
in her room and then she spent hours
in the basement pretending to be dead.
I want to tell her about the blue walls

in my turret, how they almost move
in the changing light. And the fireplace,
the way it captures the candles' flames
in its black reflection
and all the windows with old
glass that ripple in the light.
Everything, even the heart,

feels blue, blue, blue. I want to tell her
it is her birthday. That I sent socks
and shirts and her favorite magazine
but her dinner arrives, and she says something

funny about being served carrots at every meal.

NOTES FROM THE DAY

Dorothy Wordsworth loses her teeth.
A train and a Russian boar.
A cedar post and a canon.
Sun, sun, sun, sun. Three chicks

and a headache. A peony close up.
Pastels in the turret. What prevents
vertigo? Not looking where the moon
will rise. Not imagining ice where

the moon should be. Like sinking in
a sandbar and giving something quiet
to the first light, such as contentment.
The wood sorrel yellows at the roadside

and the dog pisses on it.

IT WANTS TO BE A LOVE POEM

W shows up as a good moon, as a pocket
of cough drops and keys. As a blue shirt,

the one he bought on Antelope Island in
Utah, that fades each year so now looks vintage.

Maybe the coffee on my lips,
maybe the noon hour,
maybe the dog walking far behind me,

maybe this is right where I was meant to be:
with W and this house in horse country.

Memory is an expected sunrise/is a pouch/
is a road I keep turning into, passing

the same cow. I am a bad decision.
W doesn't say as much, but I know

I don't know how to love. I spend
afternoons rifling through clover.

This week, three four-leafs. Whatever
works, I tell W, and keep searching.

WHEN WE KNEW

On the walk today, a man looked in
car windows to see his reflection
and sometimes he had to get nose
to nose with himself. He said something
about some motherfucker.

I'm on the phone with mom. She says I'm
avoiding her and that my brother is *in on it*
to keep her ill. A better poet would look
up the history of dementia.

Galen wrote it was caused
by a lack of "natural
warmth" and by poor diet.
For him, diet meant "lifestyle," not
food. From Plato: "the ethics of the soul
follow the temperaments of the body."
Some early Greeks thought
it was caused by a black bile or by
a chill. I wonder if mom sniffed something

and some bug crawled into her nasal
cavity and then lodged into her brain
and died then an inky black bile
leaked from the bug's body and filled

her until it came out of her backside,
and that is where a neighbor found her
in a bed of her own diarrhea with a blanket
pulled up to her nose to keep out the chill.

WHAT ISN'T MAKING SENSE

The large cat with the smallest meow
and other delicate treats. I've just now

noticed how much mom's lost dentures figure
into the equation. A friend carries her mother's

ashes to the Feast of All Souls. Mine enters
a nursing home. There is too much sun

behind the curtains. What is the night of soul?
How many rose heads can a palm cup?

I want a picture of me and the dog
and the pond all in one shot, I tell

W and then pose. I want to know
what to know. The priest asks about

the four-legged children. A fact: some
water is holy. Another: land fracking

in Pennsylvania. I've driven up to a past
where I don't remember much.

A NECESSARY MOTION

As if sanity hid in my hands
all this time, small as a chickadee
egg and messy like a plum.

HOLDING PATTERN

Insert fluff in the breeze here.
Say something rough as an adverb.

Allow an answer to lodge itself into tomorrow.
Saw it out, I said, before something else departed.

I could see the corner of something spent.
Concerning this, what should be asked?

The greenest scarf in the crispest snowbank.
A kind of movement too quick to catch.

The throat clogs to show how to want.
Hold it in. Even the waste. See what good it does.

In the hollow of a log or an attic, place something
tender. Maybe it will ripen overnight.

PORTRAITS

I dream mom is alone in her bed and wasting.
No nurse will help. One even says: *I can't.*

She's too big. But she is all bone.
I dream a green apple trades for mom's face.

Her finger points. So often her eyes are cut out.
She has drumsticks for hair. And each of her

days are many handed like Durga.
Before she went into the nursing home,

mom shoved takeaway boxes inside her stove.
Each full of food and ready to rot.

In the dream, a cheek kisses a cheek
in the mirror. A pink glove expects a child's hand,

which is my hand, but I am no longer a child.

Birds arrive often. I remember an assignment
from school: collage who you are.

Which body part has an opinion today?
the nurse asks. It is late afternoon

and worms hieroglyph the sidewalk.
A centipede catches between glass and screen.

In the painting there is a swimmer
or a disembodied head. In one dream:

the back of an owl. In another: a cat feeds
its litter. In my hands a husk bends back

like cricket legs and the cob bears its chest.

WHAT NEXT

The Jerusalem cricket is not from Jerusalem
nor is it a cricket. But if buried with mom

it would feed on her. The work of bugs could
be so particular like that of the Caribbean monk

seal nasal mite. The problem? When the monk
seal became extinct the mite followed. Mom calls.

Her toenails grow long as beans. She falls often
in the kitchen. She eats eggs when she remembers

to eat eggs. The washing machine does not drain.
Many things fall off this world. I am thinking

of the Rocky Mountain Locust, of the Polynesian
tree snail, of the Pigtoe and Pearly Mussel. Mom,

too, will go and I hope the Jerusalem cricket
will follow. Meanwhile, her mind cracks

like a knuckle. She eats peaches with both her
hands and allows the juice to stain her shirt.

FIRST DAYS OF SPRING

Tonight my dead father will kill my mom.
I ask her how. *Off the roof*, she says.

Some boys turn all the clocks in her apartment
back two hours. She has been "hanging on

by her nails," the nurse says. I stay away
and call less often. I repeat *bad daughter*

as if it were just another fact like
the weather. But still I wake early

and unsettled. Some night, I want to tell
mom, the dog will come. It will open

its mouth and cover her jaw with its own.
It will suck her soul as if from a straw

before jumping out the window and running
through the night and into the moon.

HEJINIAN AND ARMANTROUT TALK ABOUT THE TOPICAL POEM ONLINE

I take breaks to look out the window
to see what the dog sees. Every motion

delights us. I have come to the point that
a tea cozy is something I long for as well

as a quilt torn in many places and a pair
of slippers stained and stretched so loose

my feet can barely contain them. For what
use is "use" if we don't follow an object's

story all the way through? Right now, children
separate from their parents at the border

and California burns. Crisis everywhere. Some
afternoons mom knows her mind is going, has

gone. She says, "where are the words?"

DAD EVERYWHERE

"I saw something strange," mom says.
A man unconscious in the hallway.

She looked into the man's mouth.
And there, she said, was dad's teeth.

"I'd recognize them anywhere," she said.
At five, I watched mom's teeth

get pulled—one by one—
to prepare for dentures. Mom said

I made the most awful faces. So even
now when it rains I imagine teeth

falling. The creek fills with them and piles
like gravel on shore. I could grab fistfuls.

BORROWING

There are other writers' images
like the essayist's hummingbird
caught in her uncle's hands and

when he opened them there
was the broken beak. This is
the damage I have done to W,

leaving him again and again.
But that isn't right. The hummingbird
will starve for real. Another poet

would use a clarifying image
here. I am most interested
in the stories about power, especially

the ones where *no one saw it coming*.
I'm staying in a noisy neighborhood
where trains and traffic drown out

the birds. Inexplicably a neighbor
sometimes drags a chain about his
yard. I wish I were Caravaggio

searching for a human saint.

BIRDS AND OTHER THINGS

A friend sends a poem about a dying dog
and I think about the kind of feeling that
happens in my gut that W once

identified for me as dread and how
the poem also describes a goat's scream
when its kid has been taken. Young

billies on some dairy farms, I look up,
are killed after birth since they can't
produce milk. When I visited

the quail farm, of course I remembered
the one my dad kept in the basement
to train the bird dogs, that one quail

alone in the dark. I want to make
a statement here. Something
about marriage, maybe. Or about loss.

But I choose a bowl-full of quail eggs
and learn I should keep them "natural,"
meaning as the moment they

were laid, not cleaned, and in this
way they do not need to be pasteurized.
Clean them only right before you eat,

the farmer says, and be sure to crack
them in a bowl first in case of any oddities.
W is with me. He just came from the eye

doctor. Bifocals, he says, I am getting old.
And I say something about how nice it is
to get old together and he says something

about how the quail eggs look like stones.
The friend sends me another poem.
This one about not being able to name

the birds she hears at 4 a.m. when she
first opens her door to her garden. I've
told students again and again how

important it is to name things. Be
like Adam, I tell them, name the animals
and trees and streets and towns and

countries. It's your job as a poet to do so.
But there is something far more honest
in this admission of not being able

to name even the most often things we
hear. There is a fan in the window, no air
conditioning, just like my childhood

home in Pennsylvania. The fan is loud
like my mind. Yesterday I learned that
when I was pregnant my son's cells

passed into my bloodstream and from
then on I was two people instead of
one. Also that generational trauma is

real and studies prove this with mice
and mice offspring, but when I tell W
about this, he shakes his head in

disbelief. I remember the book
about the woman who pretended
to be mentally ill in order to get

into an asylum and report
on the conditions. Nurses would line
the patients up and stick one body

after another into the same tub
of cold water. Nellie Bly. 1887.
"Nearly all night long I listened to

a woman cry about the cold and beg
for God to let her die," wrote Nellie.
In the car today I listen to a psychologist

tell me that the mind believes what
it is told. "So why not tell the mind good
things?" says the psychologist.

Mind, I say, *you are not scared.* But
even as I say this slowly and deliberately
a thought underneath says *I am scared.*

I am very, very scared. Life coils in the corner and shakes. Mom is no longer mom. She lost her dentures two months ago. Each day

she gnaws at her food with her gums.

ANOTHER PORTRAIT

I found I could say things with color, says O'Keefe.
In the morning grass, the dog sniffs the rabbit scat

and I run through facts in my brain to sooth me
through the afternoon—as mom settles

into the nursing home. Crows remember human faces.
Cows can hold grudges. Kiki Smith: I spend hours

taking photos of the sidewalk.
Loss comes in other ways too.

Each Friday, the garbage truck lifts the can
and I love watching the entire week's refuse drop.

Chickens have good memories. Pigs can't sweat.
Don't ask what the work is, says Eva Hesse.

Mom's hands are the same hands of her
forty-year-old self. Which means they are

the same hands that first touched me when I was
born. Now they curl at her chest. We had

learned quickly in the family farmhouse that mice are
always hungry. Soon the farmhouse will sell;

I will be in one space and mom in another. A friend
says to "find my people." All tuna are nomadic.

Ann Hamilton says, One doesn't arrive
by necessarily knowing where one is going.

I eat vegetable. I eat soy. Don't hurt
the animals, please. At least not when

there is enough loss. Right now mom is leaving.
Actually, she has long been gone.

And the dog opens its mouth to the shit.

DIVINE MERCY SUNDAY

I want to read a happy poem and have
a dog at my feet, a good soup on the stove.

Outside pink-purple petals fill
the gutter below the azaleas. Today

a priest asks, *what do you doubt?*
It is the anniversary of Jesus appearing

to the disciples and when Thomas distrusts.
Far later, 1370, Jesus exchanges his heart

with St. Catherine. Her companions testify
to her wound. *Each in the cell of himself,*

I recall. Or in the field feel the fullness
of field. In the *New York Times,* I learn cells

are self-destructive. Like cannibal level
self-destructive. *Every three days, you*

basically have a new heart, says Dr.
Cuervo. Good news when I fear the end

of the marriage. At the pond, turtles carry
their shells. St. Catherine says, *Build yourself*

a spiritual cell you can take with you.
Whose heart can I exchange for my own?

BOX

after Joseph Cornell

This is something to keep your wonders in,
says the box. A bird or two with a number

on each wing. A diagram of a molar
next to an actual molar pulled long ago.

A picture of a goldfish on its side.
Puppet strings and a blue dress.

This is how we hold it together,
says the box. A robin carries the dog's

fur into the woods. Neighbors cut a trail
from their door to the road and leave

the rest of the grass uncut. For environmental
reasons, they say, and I leave enamored

with the neighbors. There is a string hanging
from the shirt. This is what you can cut,

says the box. Let's create a porch and a view,
says the box. And if we balance two balls

in the tree over there? Or center the crosshairs
of a rifle scope on the doll's face?

Empty the teapot into the pile of feather, says
the box. This box is full of gray feet and hooked
beaks. Of rust that stains my white skirt orange.

NON-MIND

Children run nearly into the street,
Stopping just at the edge of the sidewalk.

I've never known a love like that.

*Body teaches interdependence; body teaches
impermanence,* says the psychologist.

Everything I ate this morning is still inside of me.

In the interview with the famous poet,
there is a lot of placing an ear on the earth.

Just yesterday a black snake crossed the street
and then I could no longer go outside.

So I go to the market.

A lady with a silk scarf over her hair says
What a fine skirt! A mother with a child

wrapped in a blanket tells me how to
keep my house plants alive.

In a store window, I see myself and the sky
behind me. It's me. A "me."

(I have to tell myself this as if I weren't there.)

Then I cross the street, and it
feels like running toward something.

ABSTRACTION

The Buddhist teacher tells me
that mind in Chinese translates
into heart-mind. Ram Dass
says something about the breath
in the breath. All of this
is about ego and distance
and distance from ego.
The smallest bit of water
in the snowy mountainside
that looks aqua in the light.

An artist describes abstraction
as being freed from
representation. A heart
need not be represented
by the heart. And so on.
Kandinsky and expressing
the inner life in nonmaterial
ways. So that this upside

down "u" that looks like "n"
next to several other "n"
shapes can be a soul
or a fear or the edges
of a body among bodies
but also the knobs of
Kentucky that teach me
the psychology of color
and form. I should move

inward here and say
something about why
I can't stay asleep
knowing mom calls
for the nurses all night
to help save her from
my father and the men
who keep breaking
in with their guns
wanting to "steal
all of the meat." She
laughs when she tells

me this. "They couldn't
have killed us all," she
says. "There are too
many of us." What I
am trying to understand
is if the mind is concrete
or abstract. Is it the black
bird or a suggestion of
a black bird in that one
squiggle of a pencil
mark on page four?

Mom and I talk
for half an hour, trying
to make sense of all
these realities until
she tires of me
and my questions

and says "thank you
for calling" in such
an oddly formal way
that I get off the phone
and open the backdoor
to the woods and
cannot find a single
bird among the trees
not one thing to
hold all of the emotions
I wish to transfer
into some form
outside of my own.

ACKNOWLEDGEMENTS

Deep gratitude to David Roderick. And such thanks to Jan Fortune. Thanks to the Dean's office for Northern Kentucky University's College of Arts and Sciences Professional Development Award and for the English Department and Chair John Alberti for funding for a workshop with Martha Collins and a workshop with Jay Deshpande. Always all my love and gratitude go to Joe W and Devon J and mom. And I can't thank Paul Kareem Tayyar enough for believing in my work. My NKU creative writing colleagues, Jessica and Steve and Michelle, I thank you for being there. Thanks to Joan Ferrante for always believing. And thanks to Missy and Trish and all the studio-mates in the Castle Compound. And thanks always to Mary Ann Samyn. And, maybe most importantly, thanks to Fergus for the long walks and cuddles and for being the best dog ever.

NOTES

"When We Knew" contains quotes from "The Ancient History of Dementia" by Niki Papavramidou.

The essayist mentioned in "Borrowing" is Aurelia Kessler and her amazing essay is "El Valle, 1991: An Early Lesson in Strength and Fragility."

The first friend mentioned in "Birds and Other Things" is poet Missy Brownson Ross. She is the one who sent the poem about the dying dog. And the other friend is the poet and artist Patricia Baldwin Seggebruch who sent me one of her beautiful original poems that mentions her morning garden and not knowing the names of the birds. She is also the keeper of the quail and the author of the quail egg advice. The psychologist mentioned is Marisa Peer. I read about generational trauma in Jane Ratcliffe's "What Will We Do for Fun Now?"

"Box" is inspired by Vasko Popa.

The psychologist mentioned in "Non-Mind" is Lopön Charlotte Z. Rotterdam from an interview in *Lion's Roar*. The famous poet is Jack Gilbert from an interview in *American Poetry Review.*

KELLY MOFFETT is an Associate Professor of English at Northern Kentucky University. She has three collections of poetry and one chapbook and one more collection on its way through Salmon Poetry. Her work has appeared in journals such as *Colorado Review, Copper Nickel, Rattle, Cincinnati Review,* and *Laurel Review.* She is a recipient of a Fulbright Core Scholar Award, five Kentucky Foundation for Women Grants, and three residencies in Ireland. WWW.KELLYMOFFETT.COM

CPSIA information can be obtained
at www.ICGtesting.com
Printed in the USA
LVHW090059281021
701667LV00010B/661

9 781733 784832